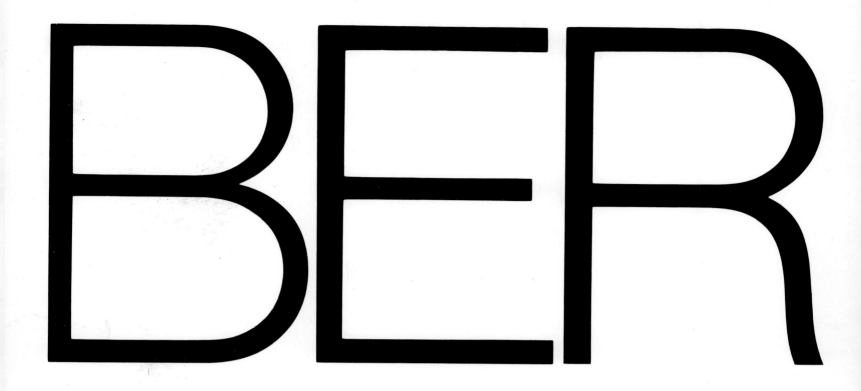

BER

INTRODUCTION

BERLIN

HISTORIC BERLIN

THE BERLINERS

THE STREETS OF BERLIN

THE CULTURAL METROPOLIS

THE GREEN CITY

THE UNITED CITY

Published by Gallery Books
A Division of W H Smith Publishers Inc.
112 Madison Avenue
New York, New York 10016

Produced by
Brompton Books Corp.
15 Sherwood Place
Greenwich, CT 06830

ISBN 0-8317-0752-6

Printed in Hong Kong

10 9 8 7 6 5 4 3 2

The authors and publishers would like to thank the Zenit
picture agency and the undernoted photographers who
supplied the photographs for pp 129-136.

Andreas Schoelzel pp 129, 131, 135.
Paul Langrock pp 132-3, 134.
Metin Yilmaz p 136.

To my dear
    friend Paul,

Remember the adventure in
Berlin, Germany during Easter Week of 1997?
I will never forget the compassion, grace, and
affection with which you handled my dilemma,
"Get over it!" I love you too!
I've really enjoyed getting my camera & photos
back. Come see me often.
                                        Much love,
                                        Carmen 6/21/97

PHOTOGRAPHY	GÜNTER SCHNEIDER
TEXT	ROLF STEINBERG
TRANSLATION	MITCH COHEN
DESIGN	MARTIN BRISTOW GÜNTER SCHNEIDER

GALLERY BOOKS
An imprint of W.H. Smith Publishers Inc.
112 Madison Avenue
New York, New York 10016

Between the two Berlins, the ugly tapeworm of the Wall eats its way through the sea of houses. On the Eastern side, the approaches were formerly almost perfectly secured against escape attempts. On the Western side, the four-meter-high concrete wall is intermittently covered with graffiti and surreal spray paintings.

The 'State Border of the GDR' as a work of Pop Art! In divided Berlin, reality was always close to absurdity – and vice versa. The two Berlins also exist a third time, as the grown halves of a larger whole: simply as Berlin, which, as image and as reality, is much more than the sum of its parts. Despite their differing social systems, the two Berlins are interconnected in many ways, like Siamese twins. On both sides of the Wall people continue to regard themselves, above all, as Berliners.

In the beginning, too, it was a double city. Cölln and Berlin, first mentioned in documents in 1237 and 1244 respectively, faced each other across a ford in a river as frontier trading posts in Germany's 'Wild East.' In the 15th century, the Prince Electors of Brandenburg made their home in the medieval trading city against the will of the inhabitants. Frederick the Great (1740-86), under whose government Prussia rose to be a great power in the European world of dynastic states, also gave Berlin the first trappings of a capital city by turning Unter den Linden into an impressive center. His successor crowned the western exit of the new boulevard with the Brandenburg Gate in 1791, from then on the emblem of the royal city of Prussia, which had about 170,000 inhabitants at the time.

On the same spot one hundred years later, we find a completely different Berlin. In the meantime it rose to be the physical and power center of the second German Empire and developed with unprecedented dynamism into a metropolis and the largest industrial city on the continent. Between 1871 and 1914, mass immigration swelled the population from 830,000 to over two million. The increasingly wealthy middle classes moved beyond the confines of the city limits into the better districts of the 'New West,' with the Kurfürsten-damm as its center. On the eve of World War I, the contrast increased grossly between the mass misery of the proletariat in the hopelessly overcrowded workers' districts in Berlin's north and east and the monarchical pomp of the Kaiser's Berlin. On November 9, 1918, workers and soldiers marched with the red flag of revolution to the Hohenzollern palace on the Spree. The old order collapsed.

In the fifteen years of the Weimar Republic, Berlin turned into a modern, fast-paced, 20th-century metropolis. Its political and administrative make-up have been transformed by the integration of surrounding towns and rural communities. In a total area of 883 square kilometers, as much as today's Munich, Frankfurt, and Stuttgart put together, the united community of Greater Berlin emerged in 1920. Its population grew in the thirties to about four million, making it the third largest city in the world, after New York and London. Feverish changes, unemployment, and increasing political radicalism charac-terized the atmosphere in the capital. In the eyes of posterity, the Berlin of the twenties is glorified to a Babylon of Modernism: an exciting, sharp-tongued, uninhibited, cosmopolitan city, cultivating creative spirits like a greenhouse and drawing the entire world's avant-garde to the 'Romanische Café' near the Memorial Church. Whether in theater, film, music, painting, literature, or the press, Berlin gleamed with new ideas in all artistic and intellectual fields. In its time, it was the undoubted cultural capital of Europe. Its international strength of personality vanished practically overnight when the Nazis came to power in 1933; the German-Jewish cultural elite scattered to the four winds.

When strolling along the Kurfürstendamm, now as then Germany's best-known boulevard, enjoying the charm of Berlin's green spaces in the Tiergarten or on the Pfaueninsel, or taking pleasure in each other's company in an Old Berlin tavern, the past is difficult to remember. It was the war that Hitler loosed upon the world from Berlin and which he lost in its rubble in 1945 that led to Germany's division: to the East, the Soviets; to the West, the Americans, British, and French.

Greater Berlin, or, more precisely, what was left of it under 75 million tons of rubble, became a special region under the joint administration of all four powers. They wanted to govern Germany together from here. The co-operation soon disintegrated under the threat of new global political conflicts. Berlin was politically divided in 1948. From then on it made headlines as the front city in the Cold War, which came to a peak on August 13, 1961 in the construction of the Wall.

It took another ten years before East and West came together in the former Allied Control Council building to defuse this source of crises with a new Four Powers' Agreement in which both sides accepted the current international situation in and around Berlin as a *modus vivendi*. Additional agreements on a national level normalized this co-existence in practical matters. For example, they improved transit traffic with West Germany and visits across the border within the city.

Although living in two different political worlds, people on both sides of the Wall nevertheless continued to regard themselves above all as Berliners. When, on the night of 9-10 November 1989, they stormed the border crossing points, spontaneous scenes of fraternization occurred everywhere.

For forty long years of German history, Berlin was the incarnation of the tragedy of a divided nation in a divided continent. Now, with the barrier wall gone and the democratic process in the GDR as good as irreversible, the city's absurd double existence has ended.

On the agenda is the further development of the two Berlins to merge into the center of a greater urban area. The new region of Berlin could quickly grow to five or six million inhabitants once the shot of Western capital into the East German economy unfolds its dynamism.

Halfway between Paris and Moscow, with direct connections to Bonn, Brussels and London, as well as to Warsaw, Praque and Vienna, Berlin has a natural role as meeting place and fulcrum in the common house of Europe. Its rebirth will demonstrate to the world what the changes in the East mean for the West and vice versa.

People living in Berlin have always responded much more sensitively to every shift in climate that could disturb the political balance. A latent tension ensures that life in the city is never boring or tedious. Even people who, for one reason or another, are biased against everything German, make an exception in their affection for Berlin.

BERLIN

'How could anyone ever come up with the idea of founding a city in the middle of all that sand?' wondered the French novelist Stendhal, when he came to the Prussian capital in 1806 as an officer of the Napoleonic occupation. Looking out from a viewpoint downtown over the irregular sea of houses, crossed by highways, waterways, rails, and industrial plants, spreading seemingly endlessly into the Markish plains, we may ask ourselves the same thing. Like a patchwork quilt, this huge concentration of humanity is composed of a colorful combination of eight formerly separate large towns as well as 59 different townships and 27 great estates. The Regional Reform of 1920 brought them together under their old names in the 20 administrative districts of Greater Berlin. There are about 45 kilometers between the easternmost and westernmost city limits. The North-South limits are 38 kilometers. Such distances keep the city constantly on the move, even in its halved state. Berlin tempo is just as proverbial for street traffic as for the temperament of the inhabitants, which has little in common with either South German placidity or North German phlegmatism.

On the map of Europe, we find Berlin in the North German Plain between the rivers Elbe and Oder on a similar latitude to London. After the war, a few artificial hills built of many millions of tons of rubble were added to the few natural elevations within the city. Together with tall buildings and television towers they form the skyline of modern Berlin. We look in vain for a towering monument indicating the historical origins of the city. While Roman cities in the Empire's West were already building their medieval cathedrals, just a few plain brick churches stood on the Spree. Surrounded by swamps and meager, sandy soil, without mineral resources or other advantages, Berlin was never more than provincial boondock in the first 500 years of its history. But at the end of the 19th century it emerged like a parvenu among the great metropoles of Europe. Cometlike, the young capital of the Reich caught up in a few decades to a point that the traditional capitals had taken centuries to reach.

Berlin cannot look back over the grandiose past of a Rome, a Vienna, or a Paris. Instead, it has kept some of the original freshness of a border and pioneer city.

15 A pair of statues by K F Schinkel on the former Palace Bridge, framed by the cupola of the Berlin Cathedral and the TV-Tower at Alexanderplatz

17 Brandenburg Gate with the Quadriga at night. In the background the Reichstag (the former German Parliament)

18-19 Aerial view into East Berlin with Brandenburg Gate and the historical boulevard Unter
den Linden, once the street of the Prussian
Kings

20-21 A good example, from the Neukölln district, of how the Wall cut the city in half

22 From lookout platforms like this one at Pots-
damer Platz, visitors used to go to look over the
Wall (top), which, on the western side, has long
been employed by painters and graffiti artists
as an open-air gallery (bottom)

23 The sight of the so-called Death Strip on the
eastern side of the wall reveals its character as
a frontier guarded by border troops, where
shootings used to occur. Memorials and
Crosses of Remembrance like this one at Ber-
nauer Straße are reminders of the fatal trage-
dies of refugees, of whom, in the past, more
than 75 have lost their lives (bottom)

24 Parade of the three Western Allies on the
Street of 17th June

25 Double Guards at the Soviet Memorial in
Tiergarten, symbolizing the still valid Four-
Power-Status of Berlin

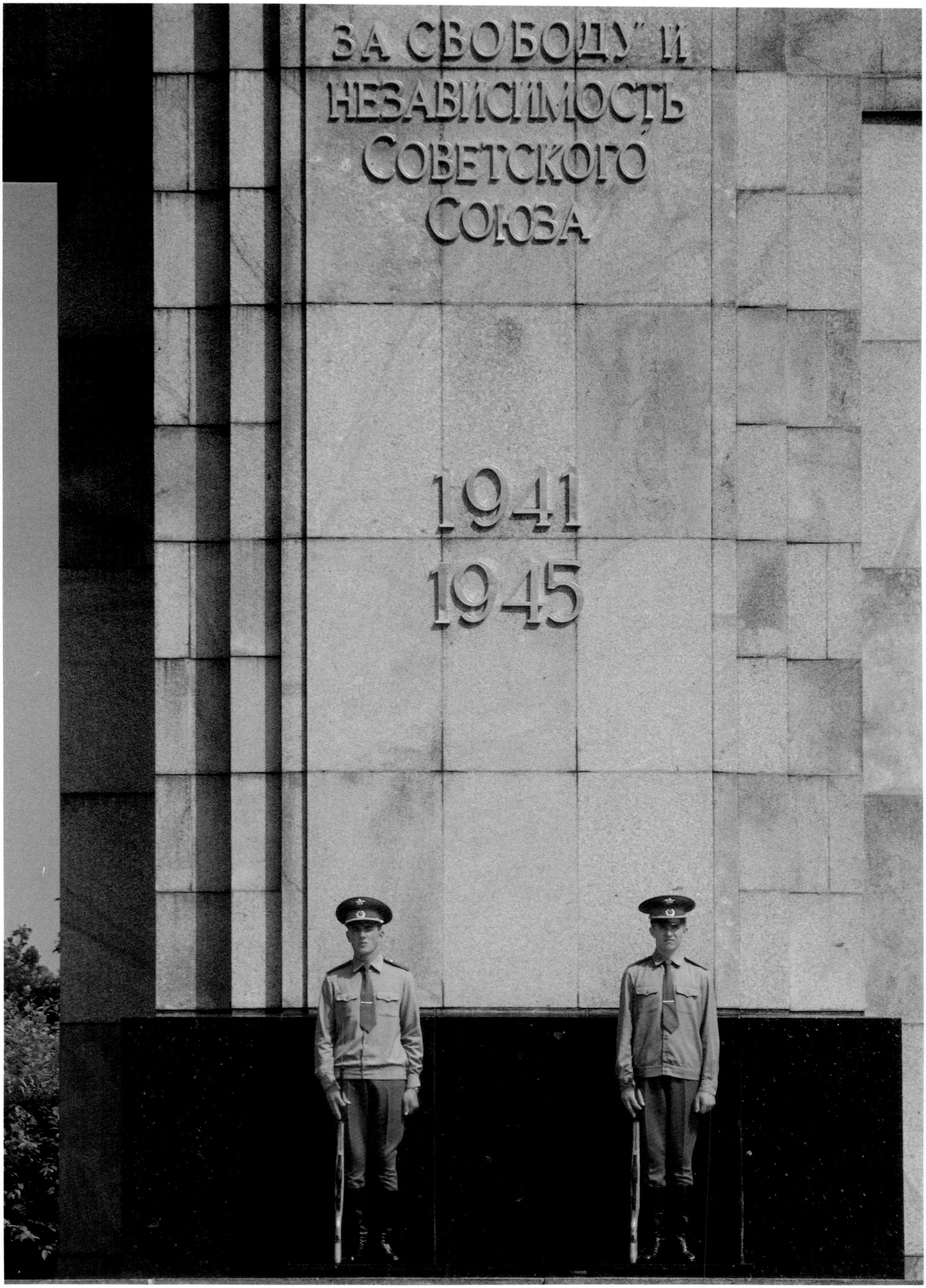
ЗА СВОБОДУ И
НЕЗАВИСИМОСТЬ
СОВЕТСКОГО
СОЮЗА
1941
1945

26 The Bismarck Monument and the gilded figure of Victory on top of the Victory Column at Großer Stern, Tiergarten: two witnesses to the former national glory in the days of Imperial Berlin

27 These two huge statues from the days of Nazi-Germany have been left standing in the Olympic Stadium

28-29 Open-air concert with Pink Floyd in front of the Reichstag (the former Parliament Building), close to the sector boundary; in the background the East Berlin skyline with the TV-tower

30 Divine service in the Memorial Church

31 A Synagogue in West Berlin

*32 Musical show at the Friedrichstadt-Palast,
East Berlin's international tourist attraction*

33 Scene from the cabaret La vie en rose, *the smaller counterpart in West Berlin's Europa-Center*

HISTORIC BERLIN

Through the centuries, Berlin has been rebuilt from scratch again and again. The master builders never felt constrained from scrapping what already stood. Even during the reconstruction following the war, the tendency to demolish rather than restore what had been damaged continued into the sixties. Thus, in 1950, during the ideological zealotry of the Stalin era, the communist SED party had the burnt-out half-ruin of the City Palace on the Spree Island razed. In West Berlin, much long-functioning building-infrastructure was sacrificed to the Americanism of a city 'suitable for cars.' Even the ruined tower of the Kaiser Wilhelm Memorial Church in the middle of the West was to disappear.

Nonetheless, Berlin does remember its history. Both parts compete to exhibit properly the stone witnesses of the past. For centuries, Berlin's history was played out principally in the few square kilometers between the Alexanderplatz and the Brandenburg Gate, in what is now East Berlin. Restored by the East German government at a cost of billions, we find here almost all the famous architectural monuments of the periods of the Baroque, of the Rococo, and of Prussian Classicism, gathered in their old beauty in front of a backdrop of socialist state architecture. At the Linden Forum around the former Royal Court Opera (today the German State Opera), Frederick the Great's constructions dominate. A few paces away on Museum Island or at the former Gendarmenmarkt, we find the most celebrated buildings of Karl Friedrich Schinkel (1781-1841), whose genius completed classical Berlin's 19th-century reputation as a new Athens on the Spree. We look back at the Berlin of the Middle Ages and Renaissance in the 'new' Old City, which huddles at Berlin's cradle around the Nikolai Church on the right bank of the Spree.

In West Berlin, an impressive example of Prussian architectural art remains in Charlottenburg Palace. This last great palace from the time of the Hohenzollerns is considered one of the most beautiful examples of the Baroque in all of North Germany.

35 Brandenburg Gate seen from the east

37 The 'new' old town around the Nikolai-Church, the medieval cradle of Berlin

38-39 Evening mood at the rebuilt Gendarmenmarkt, now called Platz der Akademie (Academy Square). In the foreground Schinkel's Schauspielhaus (State Theater), behind it the older French Cathedral

...CVS GVLIELMVS III STVDIO ANTIQVITATIS OMNIGENAE ET ARTIVM LIBERALIVM MVSEVM CONSTITVIT MDCC...

40 East Berlin upholds the heritage left by Schinkel. The neo-Gothic Church of Friedrich-werder, for decades a ruin, has been restored too. In front of it, on a pedestal, the statue of Freiherr von Stein, the great Prussian reformer of the early 19th century

41 Mounted on a charger, Frederick the Great on what used to be Berlin's most stately boulevard, Unter den Linden. The equestrian statue by Christian Rauch is ranked as a masterpiece of Prussian Classicism.

42 Schinkel's marked sense of classical pro-
portions governs the broad aspect of the tem-
ple façade of the Old Museum

43 Soldiers of the GDR-People's Army doing
the goose-step outside Schinkel's New Guard,
which today serves as a memorial to the victims
of fascism and militarism

44-45 The old city of Berlin, today part of East Berlin, extends along both banks of the River Spree

46 The interior of the Nikolai-Kirche, the oldest building of the city. Today it houses an exhibition of Berlin's history from 1237 until the end of the Thirty Years' War in 1648

47 Classicism, historicism, and socialism make up the architectural picture of East Berlin's city centre

48-49 Charlottenburg Palace in West Berlin
with its baroque garden

50 The White Room in Charlottenburg Palace,
a splendid example of Prussian rococo

51 Spandau Citadel, a 16th-century fortress
surrounded by water, guards the confluence of
the rivers Spree and Havel

THE BERLINERS

The legendary original Berliners, the first colonists, made their way from as far away as Flanders and the lower Rhine into the unpopulated wilderness between the Havel and the Spree. And so it has continued.

In the 17th and 18th centuries, Berlin rejuvenated its always stagnating population figures with Protestant religious refugees from various European countries, among them 5,000 French Huguenots. At the end of the 19th century, the unemployed rural population of the eastern agricultural provinces streamed by the hundred thousands into the industrial metropolis, which was growing much too rapidly. Labor was the most important raw material. Today, with about 150,000 new Turkish inhabitants, West Berlin is the largest Turkish city outside of Turkey. Berlin – one of its few traditions – was always a city of immigrants: a little America, where one could shake the dust from his shoes, but also where a newcomer had to fight hard to sustain himself.

According to a famous saying of Goethe's, 'an audacious breed of people' thrives on the Spree, who have distinguished themselves for their energy, quick senses, and quick tongues. A contemporary comparison sees the Berliners as the New Yorkers of Central Europe, in that every second Berliner was born elsewhere. In contrast to provincial areas, this does not affect whether one 'belongs' to Berlin: being or becoming a Berliner is not a question of descent, but of mentality. Berlin's dry wit expresses itself in a quick, sober – simply typically Berlin – way of speaking and thinking. The notorious Berlin humor lies on the same wave-length. It often sounds more biting than is intended and contains a large measure of irony. The Berliners' talent for seeing the funny side of even the most unpleasant aspects of life is undisputed. The many jokes about the Wall formerly heard in the East are an example. One of the last of these jokes reported that all Chinese were being required to leave East Berlin. The reason? They always wanted to take their Sunday stroll on the Wall!

53 Curious West Berliners crowding in on an American 'Raisin Bomber' from the time of the airlift in 1948-49

55 Pert, pretty, and fashionable – the 'Berlinerin'

56-57 *Berliners like all sorts of open-air events*

58 *The trade in antiques thrives in West Berlin. Here a vase is changing hands*

59 *Fashion show at the Radio Tower*

60 *A juggler in the summer city*

61 *A break during a stroll*

62-63 *Down-to-earth and jovial: a typical Berlin publican*

64 The punk girl and the law

65 A hurdy-gurdy idyll in a Berlin backyard

66 A keeper of Berlin's zoological garden

67 Turkish Berliners in a mosque

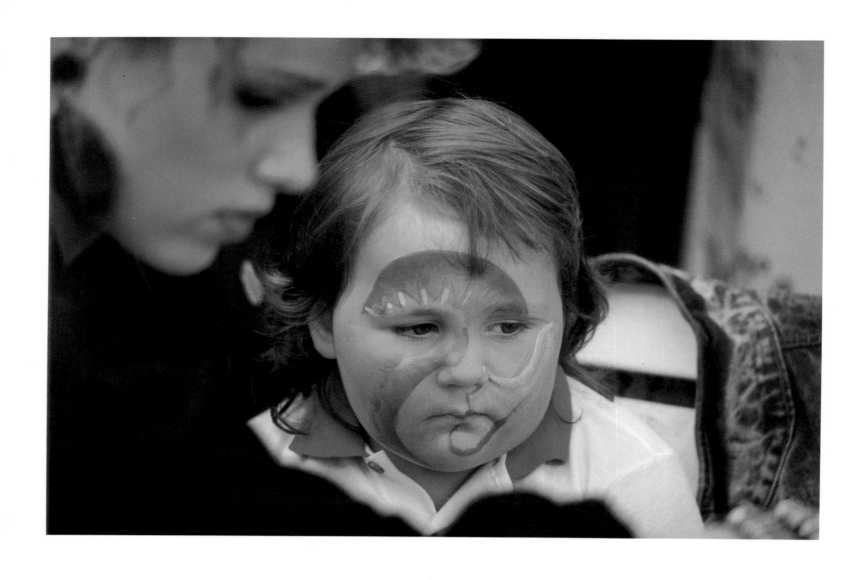

68 Children at the Jokers' Party on Los
Angeles Square outside the Steigenberger
Hotel

69 One of the youngest demonstrators at the
May Day parade in East Berlin

*70 An East Berlin block of flats on a national
holiday*

*71 An elderly married couple at the trotting
course in Mariendorf*

72 The ferryman of the Pfaueninsel (Peacock Island), one of the most popular places for outings in and around West Berlin

73 Face of a young girl who wants to be 'different'

74 Crazy styling is back in fashion

75 Portrait artist in East Berlin's historical Nikolai Quarter

THE STREETS OF BERLIN

As an urban living space, Berlin can best be compared with a collage. A drive through the labyrinth of streets resembles an expedition through different continents, where one is constantly making new discoveries. Berlin in Berlin: a few streets away, it can look completely different. The *Laubenpieper* garden-plot idyll in front of a factory wall, a *Zille* courtyard full of Old Berlin second-hand goods next to a luxury hotel, here Grand Bourgeois housing in the Belle Époque style, there a loveless dwelling-silo of naked concrete: the contours and contrasts of Berlin reveal themselves in the juxtaposition of all kinds of building and life styles.

For general orientation, a stranger is usually first drawn to the Kurfürstendamm. Here, below the revolving Mercedes star atop the Europa-Center, the metropolitan heart of Berlin beats – with all that that entails. Since almost everything exists doubly in Berlin, beginning with the two City Halls, through the two zoological gardens, to the morgues, the touristic equivalent for East Berlin has emerged at Alexanderplatz, barely ten kilometers away as the crow flies.

However, most Berliners don't live in either of these downtown areas. In the various inner suburbs or further out, in the individual neighborhoods, we find the Berlin of functioning, everyday life. Thus, when you get to know them, the Berliners turn out to be Charlottenburgers, Steglitzers, Spandauers, or Lichtenraders, and these names designate their own individual worlds. Each of the districts is a large town in its own right with its own town hall, coat-of-arms, shopping area, and its own distinctive social structure. The smaller neighborhoods vary in their special local color and their inhabitants. Grunewald, for example, is synonymous with millionaire villa-owners, Britz with a municipal bus driver in a petit bourgeois suburban tract. Those who feel at home in the heavily-populated inner city live in the 'Kietz.' This is a vaguely defined area, usually around a square, which offers its inhabitants both the familiarity of a village and an urban lifestyle.

77 West Berlin: The city in the evening with the Europe Center and the Memorial Church

79 Art Nouveau façade of an upper middle-class residence with stucco ornamentation, dating from the turn of the century. Flats in such houses are much in demand again.

80-81 Living quarters dating back to the beginning of Imperial Germany (1871-73), restored at Chamissoplatz, Kreuzberg

82-83 Street Café on Kurfürstendamm

84 A popular meeting place in the city: the Globe Fountain, also known as the 'Water Dumpling'

85 Something's always going on along the Kurfürstendamm

*86-87 Congress Hall in Tiergarten with a Henry
Moore sculpture*

*88 An old Berlin working-class district, now
taken over by Turkish immigrants from Anatolia*

89 Berlin's backyards, like this one in Schöneberg, harbor many a secret

90 *Where it all began: the town seal in front of the Nikolai-Kirche in East Berlin*

91 *Formerly called Gendarmenmarkt, today Academy Square in East Berlin, one of the places typical of Berlin as it used to be*

92 'Trabants,' GDR-built two-stroke mini-cars,
line the streets of East Berlin

93 Larger than life, Karl Marx and Friedrich En-
gels, the two pillars of Communism, face the
back of the Palace of the Republic

94 The Palace of the Republic is situated where the destroyed Royal Palace used to be, on an island of the River Spree. It houses the People's Chamber (GDR-Parliament), and a small theater, and is a popular meeting place on account of its many cafés and restaurants

95 Alexanderplatz, the modern center of the
GDR-Capital, in winter

THE CULTURAL METROPOLIS

In the 19th century, even before the unification of Germany, Berlin won national importance as capital of the Muses and of German intellectual life. Today it is the leading and by far the largest cultural metropolis in German-speaking Europe. Beyond that, internationally, it plays a role as a center for the exchange of new ideas, and is mentioned in one breath with Paris, London, and New York.

The lively, versatile cultural offerings are a big part of the city's attractiveness as a place to live or visit, whereby West Berlin shines particularly as a city of music, festivals, and museums. Beyond that, and unique in Germany, is its constantly experimenting alternative Scene, which, outside the pale of the state theaters, simultaneously responds spontaneously to and helps to create the spirit of the age. In former factory halls in Kreuzberg, old ballrooms, café-theaters, and other widely distributed sites, over a hundred independent groups stage notable demonstrations of talent, as well as the occasional flop.

The program calendar lists more than a hundred theater and music performances for the weekend. The palette of possibilities is almost too much to choose from, when one also considers the many films, art exhibitions, literary readings, workshops, and other events. West Berlin has about one hundred galleries. A trip taking in only the most important art museums would take days. And almost the whole year is taken up by festivals. The annual offering includes the International Film Festival, the Theater Meeting, fall Music and Theater Festival Weeks, and finally the Jazz Festival. And every four years at the Horizons Festival the cultures of Asia, Africa, or Latin America come for a visit.

All of this is repeated in a smaller, state-run context in East Berlin, the cultural display cabinet of the GDR. Both sides profit from the competition between the systems, now that the aggressive rivalry between East and West has given way to constructive exchange. Moreover, both Berlins draw from a common tradition. Nonetheless, it took nearly forty years before the Berlin Philharmonic, which journeys around the entire world as ambassador of the city, was able to give its first, enthusiastically greeted concert on the other side of the Wall.

97 A visit to the old masters at Dahlem Gallery

99 The Seagull by Anton Chekhov: a scene from a production at the Schiller-Theater, one of West Berlin's three municipal theaters.

100-101 A romantic summer evening at the
open-air 'Waldbühne'

102 'Grips' (Brains) is the name of Berlin's re-
nowned Youth Theater; a scene from a production of its own musical, Line One

103 Reflections in the glass front of the National Gallery, which specializes in the art of the 19th and 20th centuries, at what has become known as the Culture Forum

104-105 The Berlin Philharmonic Orchestra in the new concert hall for chamber music

*106 In the plaster workshop, copies are made
of some of Berlin's famous sculptures*

*107 A copy of the head of the most famous
Egyptian lady of royal blood, Nefertiti, is greatly
in demand as a souvenir*

108 The Pergamon Altar on East Berlin's
Museum Island is an outstanding example of
classical Greek architecture in Asia Minor
109 Rococo interior of the German State Opera
on East Berlin's Unter den Linden. It was built
by George Wenzeslaus von Knobelsdorff in
1741-43 and contained at that time only one
seat, that of King Frederick II

THE GREEN CITY

Many an air passenger must have rubbed his eyes in astonishment when his plane came in to land at Tegel Airport: 'That's supposed to be Berlin?' He had been expecting a walled-in asphalt jungle and was greeted instead by an island within a green belt. Running through it like a broad silver ribbon is the glittering Havel where, in fine weather, hundreds of sails gleam – that too, is Berlin.

Lakes, rural areas, parks, and rivers make up about a third of the whole city area, so that Berlin can fairly claim to be the greenest metropolis in Europe. Some people refer to the city as a 'huge village.' Indeed, within its present borders it is largely made up of former villages, as can be seen by the 45 village churches which still exist in Berlin, some of them still in their traditional surroundings next to a village green.

Berlin's spacious outlying districts offer the city dweller a multitude of places for outings where, at the sight of a creaking windmill or a peacock spreading its tail, he might feel as if he'd gone away to the country. There are also many public footpaths for hiking. One fifth of West Berlin is covered by woods, in which you might encounter wild boars or foxes but never meet another human soul for hours.

The most attractive aspect of the countryside surrounding Berlin, the Brandenburg March, is the wooded and aqueous scenery of the River Havel which flows past the western periphery of the city for 30 kilometers, forming a chain of lakes with picturesque islands and bays. At this recreational and aquatic paradise, stretching from Tegel to lake Wannsee, it gets a bit crowded on a summer's weekend.

Others might prefer the view over the river out of season, the quiet charm which gives a hint of the vast expanse stretching east.

111 Houseboats on the Landwehrkanal in the
Tiergarten

113 Yearning for the open air

114-115 *View of the River Havel*

116-117 *Sun worshippers at Wannsee municipal beach*

118 Windsurfer on the Havel

119 Palais Pfaueninsel (Peacock Island),
Berlin's romantic jewel set in water

120 Harvester close to the Märkische Viertel.
About 30 family farms continue Berlin's rural
tradition.

121 The average Berliner likes to spend a summer Sunday at the water or in one of the many
roadhouses

122-123 Hang-gliders at the Teufelsberg

124 A melancholy morning mist over the Havel

125 Palace garden Glienicke in the winter

126-127 St Hubert's Day hunt in the Grunewald

128 Art and politics meet symbolically at the
edge of the Tiergarten. Across the honey-
colored roof of the Philharmonic Hall, we can
make out the Reichstag in the east

THE UNITED CITY

The radical developments which took place in Berlin in the few short weeks of November 1989 caught the imagination of watchers around the world and changed their lives and those of every Berliner in a breathtaking way.

Spurred on by Gorbachov's *perestroika*, the people of East Germany took their destiny into their own hands, rising up in a peaceful revolution against the Stalinist regime of coercion in the East. After the fall of the Wall which resulted, the city's perspectives for the future were opened up beyond anyone's dreams.

Under overwhelming pressure from mass protests, the new East German leadership finally rushed headlong to open the borders to the West. On the evening of November 9th – a date already memorable in German history as the anniversary of the Revolution of 1918, for Hitler's failed coup in Munich in 1923, and for the shameful Nazi pogroms of the *Reichskristallnacht* of 1938 – on this momentous Thursday evening East German television casually stated that GDR citizens were free to visit the West.

The sensational news had hardly been announced before Berliners from both sides hurried to the various crossing points along the Wall. Around 10pm the first East Berliners dashed jubilantly across the white border strip, and soon there was no stopping the tide. Berlin celebrated the happiest festival of reunion in its history.

The next morning anyone who heard the reports of the night's events had a feeling of waking up in another, no longer divided Berlin. It had become, at least in the imaginations of Berliners, one city again. It was only after this transformation that Berliners really realised how much their walled existence had confined and depressed them. After 28 years of forcible separation, they could finally move freely in their city and beyond.

Previous page: A colorful freedom demonstration in East Berlin in November 1989

Right: An astonishing transformation – East Berliners drive freely into the West

Overleaf: The Wall and the Brandenburg Gate, 10 November 1989

Left: New crossing places are quickly made

Above: A happy East Berlin family passes a border checkpoint

Overleaf: Photographs and souvenir pieces of the Wall ensure that the great events will not be forgotten